in
the
news™

ILLEGAL IMMIGRATION AND AMNESTY

OPEN BORDERS AND NATIONAL SECURITY

Janey Levy

ROSEN
PUBLISHING®

New York

Published in 2010 by The Rosen Publishing Group, Inc.
29 East 21st Street, New York, NY 10010

Copyright © 2010 by The Rosen Publishing Group, Inc.

First Edition

Library of Congress Cataloging-in-Publication Data

Levy, Janey.
Illegal immigration and amnesty: open borders and national security / Janey Levy.
    p. cm.—(In the news)
Includes bibliographical references and index.
ISBN 978-1-4358-3583-2 (library binding)
ISBN 978-1-4358-8548-6 (pbk)
ISBN 978-1-4358-8549-3 (6 pack)
1. United States—Emigration and immigration—Government policy.
2. Illegal aliens—United States. 3. Amnesty—United States. I. Title.
JV6483.L52 2010
325.73—dc22

2009020623

Manufactured in Malaysia

CPSIA Compliance Information: Batch #TWW10YA: For Further Information contact Rosen Publishing, New York, New York at 1-800-237-9932

On the cover: Clockwise from upper left: A uniformed officer from the Maricopa County (Arizona) sheriff's office accompanies an illegal immigrant arrested during a 2009 raid on a local business; in 1997, Representative Maxine Waters of California calls for granting amnesty to illegal Haitian immigrants; while some people support using border fences, such as this one, to fight illegal immigration, others warn that such fences will disrupt the migration of rare wildlife and harm the environment.

contents

Illegal Immigration and Amnesty: The Basics

Illegal immigration has been in the news a lot lately. You've probably heard people talking or even arguing about it. People debate its causes, its consequences, and the most effective way to deal with it.

With all the attention that illegal immigration has received recently, you might think it's a new problem. In fact, the place of immigration—both legal and illegal—in U.S. society has been passionately debated for centuries. The debate surrounding illegal immigration and the methods of dealing with it has been especially heated, particularly regarding a proposed solution often called amnesty. The terrorist attacks of September 11, 2001, focused more attention on illegal immigration. They made the debate more highly charged and the need for a solution more urgent. But before examining the issue further, you need to know something about the terminology, or language, and process of immigration.

Immigration Terms and Process

An immigrant is someone who moves into a country from another country with plans to stay. According to the Organisation for Economic Co-operation and Development, the United States and Canada define an immigrant as anyone who is born in (and is a citizen of) one country before coming to live in another country. That means the person remains an immigrant even after becoming a U.S. or Canadian citizen. Popularly, however, the term refers to someone who moves into a new country but remains a citizen of the old country.

Sometimes, immigrants are called aliens. "Alien" simply means someone who was born in another country. However, some people object to the term because it is often used in an insulting manner to imply that the immigrants' ancestry and culture make them unacceptably different from the people of their new country.

Legal immigrants are those who enter a new country in accordance with that country's laws. According to the U.S. Department of State, prospective immigrants must apply for a visa—a stamp placed in the individual's passport—at the American embassy or consulate in their country of origin. A visa doesn't guarantee the person entry into the United States. It simply means an official has determined that the individual meets eligibility

This man from India proudly poses for a photograph after becoming a U.S. citizen. The process leading to this moment began years earlier with his application for a visa.

requirements. Only the immigration officer at the port of entry has the authority to allow an immigrant to enter.

The visa application process can be complex and lengthy. An applicant must complete forms, pay fees, and submit photographs and proof of financial support and of vaccinations for numerous diseases. An embassy or consulate official interviews the applicant, collects finger scans, and ensures that the applicant has no criminal record.

As the term suggests, illegal immigrants are in a new country illegally. Most people think illegal immigrants are people who have entered illegally. However, people who entered legally but stayed after their visa expired, such as students or tourists whose visas permitted only a limited stay, are illegal immigrants, too. So are people who entered legally but disobeyed the visa's terms—for example, people with student visas who took jobs—and people who lied to get their visa.

Another term that you often hear in the immigration debate is "open borders." Sometimes, it simply means loosening restrictions to allow more people to immigrate legally. In discussions about illegal immigration, however, it commonly refers to a lack of border security.

Just as immigrants are sometimes called aliens, illegal immigrants are also called illegal aliens or "illegals." Some people object to those terms for the same reasons that they object to calling immigrants "aliens." Other terms applied to illegal immigrants include "undocumented workers," "undocumented immigrants," and "unauthorized immigrants."

Captured illegal immigrants are usually deported, or returned to their country of origin. This is one of the most common solutions to illegal immigration. Amnesty—forgiving illegal immigrants for their illegal acts and creating a way for them to become

An immigration officer at San Francisco International Airport checks an immigrant's passport and visa against a computer database. The officer can deny the immigrant entry if the information doesn't match.

legal immigrants—is one of the most hotly debated solutions.

What Are the Issues Surrounding Illegal Immigration and Amnesty?

So what keeps illegal immigration in the news? It's not simply that it happens. It's because its causes, consequences, and solutions are sources of controversy. The fact that these arguments have continued for years is evidence of how difficult it is for people to reach a consensus, or agreement. What are some of the specific issues that people argue about? The list below covers the main points.

- Do illegal immigrants create an economic burden by taking advantage of social services, such as food stamps, medical care, and welfare? Or do illegal immigrants contribute to the economy?
- Do illegal immigrants take jobs away from U.S. workers? Or do they take jobs American workers won't accept?
- Do illegal immigrants lead to a higher crime rate and place a burden on the prison system?
- Does the increased population resulting from illegal immigration endanger the environment of the United States?
- Do illegal immigrants contribute to the country's cultural richness? Or do they threaten the unity of U.S. society by refusing to learn English and insisting on maintaining their cultural traditions?
- Do illegal immigrants pose a terrorist threat?
- Is amnesty the best and fairest way to deal with the millions of illegal immigrants in the United States? Or is it unfair to immigrants and prospective immigrants who follow the rules? Will it encourage more illegal immigration?

• What options besides amnesty exist for dealing with illegal immigration? Should the United States simply continue to deport illegal immigrants who are caught? Are there ways to halt illegal immigration? What is the financial cost of these options?

Before examining illegal immigration and amnesty more closely, however, it's important to set the stage by briefly looking at the history of immigration in the United States. Why does knowing the history matter? Well, consider someone who has amnesia, who can't remember his or her past. That person no longer knows his or her identity. The same is true for a nation that doesn't know its history. Knowing the past can help you understand the present and separate fact from fiction in the news stories that you hear or read on illegal immigration and amnesty. For example, is it true, as people often say, that the United States is a nation of immigrants? Has the United States always welcomed immigrants? Have all immigrants been treated equally? What kinds of laws has the U.S. government passed to deal with immigration? The next chapter provides a short introduction to these issues.

A Nation of Immigrants: Immigration in U.S. History

Native Americans were in what is now the United States thousands of years before Europeans came. Theories differ about when Native Americans first appeared, but most experts agree that they arrived at least fifteen thousand years ago. Some believe it may have been much earlier. The most common theory is that people crossed a land bridge from Asia into what is now Alaska during the last ice age. At that time, much of the world's water was frozen in huge ice sheets that covered large areas of land. As a result, sea levels were lower, exposing a strip of land between Asia and Alaska.

The first Europeans to reach North America were probably the Vikings, who arrived around 1000 CE. The few settlements that they established along the eastern coast didn't last. European immigration really began in the early 1500s, following Christopher Columbus's 1492 voyage to the Americas.

Immigration into the United States, 1500 to 1965

The first European immigrants to what would become the United States were the Spanish, who established settlements in the early 1500s. About a century later, immigrants from England, France, Germany, Ireland, Wales, the Netherlands, Scotland, and Sweden arrived. Most of them came in search of economic opportunity or religious freedom.

Some who came during the 1600s didn't come by choice. Convicts from overcrowded English jails were sent to the colonies. Most Africans and Afro-Caribbeans were brought by force to serve as slaves.

During the 1700s and 1800s, most immigrants came from northern and western European countries like England, Scotland, Ireland, Wales, Germany, France, Norway, Sweden, Denmark, Switzerland, and Belgium. However, the 1848 discovery of gold in California brought a whole new group of immigrants. Tens of thousands of Chinese arrived, bringing with them culture, traditions, and language that were vastly different from those of other immigrants.

Between about 1880 and 1920, "new immigrants" from southern and eastern Europe—Italy, Poland, Hungary, and Greece—began to arrive, fleeing poverty and overpopulation. Russian and Polish Jews came to

This photograph from early 1900 shows a group of European immigrants on Ellis Island. Located in New York Harbor, Ellis Island welcomed more than twelve million immigrants between 1892 and 1954.

escape religious persecution. Mexicans fleeing war and poverty arrived. Like the earlier Chinese immigrants, these immigrants brought diverse cultures, traditions, languages, and religions.

Attitudes Toward Immigrants, 1500 to 1965

Did you know there were originally no immigration laws in what would become the United States? The borders were truly open. People simply came. However, that doesn't mean everyone received a warm welcome. Even Benjamin Franklin and Thomas Jefferson expressed concern. Franklin's attitude later changed, but he once complained that German immigrants threatened American society's unity. Jefferson worried that they wouldn't uphold the young country's republican values. George Washington, however, welcomed everyone—the poor and persecuted as well as the prosperous. In fact, most immigrants to the United States over the centuries have assimilated, enriched the nation's culture, and helped the country become what it is today.

The Naturalization Act of 1790—the first U.S. immigration law—limited citizenship to "free white persons," which was understood to mean European men. Still, all European male immigrants weren't treated equally. During the 1800s, German and Irish Catholics, southern and eastern Europeans, and Polish and Russian Jews suffered discrimination. They were considered menaces that caused increased crime and poverty, threatened liberty and property, and carried diseases.

Because Asian cultures and languages differ so radically from those of other people of the United States, Asian immigrants—especially the Chinese—endured harsh discrimination. The borders began to close with the Chinese Exclusion Act of 1882, which barred Chinese laborers. People complained that they were culturally and physically inferior, brought diseases, threatened social unity, reduced wages, and weren't Christian. Sometimes, Chinese immigrants were subjected to violent attacks.

Over the next eighty years, many immigration and citizenship laws were passed. The Naturalization Act of 1906 established uniform naturalization rules and required knowledge of English. The Immigration Act of 1917 severely limited Asian immigration, taxed immigrants, and required immigrants older than sixteen to prove their literacy. A 1924 law allowed unrestrained Western Hemisphere immigration but limited immigrants from elsewhere, especially Asia. The Immigration and Nationality Act of 1952 introduced quotas based on nationality. In 1965, amendments to the act replaced quotas with limits divided between the Eastern and Western hemispheres, ushering in a new era.

Immigration Since 1965

The Hart-Cellar Act of 1965—the law that amended the Immigration and Nationality Act of 1952—changed immigration patterns. It limited Eastern Hemisphere immigration to 170,000 annually and, for the first time, placed numerical restrictions on Western Hemisphere immigration (120,000). (Amendments in 1978 eliminated the division between hemispheres and set a worldwide

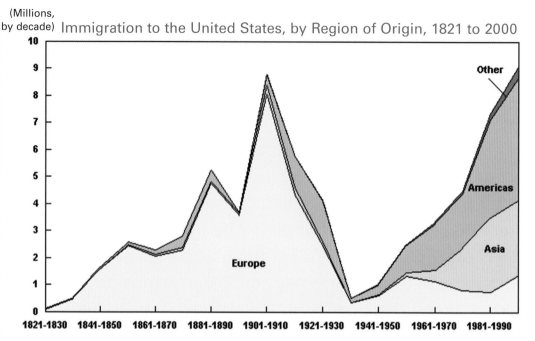

(Millions, by decade) Immigration to the United States, by Region of Origin, 1821 to 2000

As this Department of Homeland Security graph shows, the proportion of immigrants from the Americas and Asia has greatly increased since about 1940, while the proportion from Europe has decreased.

cap of 290,000.) The act also gave preference to relatives of citizens and permanent residents and to people with special skills or training needed in the United States.

Elizabeth Kolsky, an assistant professor of history at Pratt Institute in New York, says the special skills preference significantly affected what nationalities were admitted. Earlier immigrants mostly came from Europe. Kolsky notes that immigrants from India totaled about sixteen thousand in the century before Congress passed the act. However, between 1965 and 1975, nearly ninety-seven thousand Indian immigrants arrived.

According to the U.S. Department of Homeland Security's *2007 Yearbook of Immigration Statistics*, more U.S. immigrants have come from Asia and the Americas than from Europe since 1970. Roger Daniels, author of *Guarding the Golden Door: American Immigration Policy and Immigrants Since 1882*, says about 70 percent of the immigrants who entered legally in 1999 came from Asia and Latin America.

Using government figures, Daniels tracked changes in Asian immigration between 1960 and 2000. Between 1960 and 1970, China and the Philippines provided the most immigrants—about one hundred thousand each—with Japan a distant third, at about forty thousand. Between 1990 and 2000, almost 1.5 million immigrants came from the Philippines. About 1.2 million came from China. Korea, India, and Vietnam—each provided more than seven hundred thousand immigrants. Fewer than two hundred thousand came from Japan. According to the U.S. Department of State's *Report of the Visa Office 2008*, more than 176,000 Asian immigrants entered between October 1, 2007, and September 30, 2008. Most came from China and the Philippines (more than thirty thousand each), India (almost twenty-six thousand), Vietnam (nearly twenty-four thousand), and Pakistan (almost fourteen thousand).

Daniels also used government figures to show trends in legal immigration to the United States from Mexico between 1940 and 1990. Between 1940 and 1950, more than sixty thousand Mexicans entered. Between 1980 and 1990, that number surged to more than 1.6 million. According to the *Report of the Visa Office 2008*, more than ninety-one thousand Mexican immigrants entered legally between October 1, 2007, and September 30, 2008.

The *Report of the Visa Office 2008* shows that immigration to the United States from the Americas (including Mexico) totaled 205,166 from October 1, 2007, to September 30, 2008, while European immigrants totaled only about thirty-eight thousand. These figures reveal an enormous change in immigration patterns from U.S. colonial days.

Regulating Immigration Since 1965

Members of Congress didn't anticipate the changes in immigration patterns that resulted from the Hart-Cellar Act. They've proposed many immigration bills since then, but only some of them have become laws. In 1980, the annual total of immigrants allowed into the United States was reduced to 270,000. The Immigration Reform and Control Act of 1986 (IRCA) retained this cap, but relatives of citizens and permanent residents weren't included in this number. As a result, the actual number of legal immigrants admitted in 1987 was more than six

In 2005, President George W. Bush *(left)* watches as Supreme Court Justice Sandra Day O'Connor *(second from left)* swears in the new secretary of homeland security, Michael Chertoff *(third from right)*.

hundred thousand, says Willi Paul Adams, author of *The German-Americans: An Ethnic Experience*.

Against the advice of the Immigration and Naturalization Service (INS), Daniels says, Congress also included in the IRCA a visa waiver program that modified earlier laws requiring anyone who entered the country for any reason—immigrant, tourist, student, and so on—to have an appropriate visa. It waived, or set aside, the requirement for certain tourists who intended to stay for ninety days or less.

The Immigration Act of 1990 increased the number of legal immigrants allowed into the United States each year. The annual limit was set at seven hundred thousand from 1992 to 1994. Since 1995, the limit has been 675,000.

The September 11, 2001, terrorist attacks on the World Trade Center in New York City and the Pentagon in northern Virginia had an enormous impact on the government's approach to dealing with immigrants. One consequence was that controlling immigration increasingly came to be seen as a matter of national security. The federal government created a new agency: the Department of Homeland Security (DHS). The INS was abolished, and three divisions within the DHS took over its responsibilities: the U.S. Citizenship and Immigration Services (USCIS), the U.S. Immigration and Customs Enforcement (ICE), and the Border Patrol.

The terrorist attacks strongly influenced public perception of immigrants. They especially affected attitudes toward illegal immigrants, whom many Americans began to view with greater suspicion and fear. But who are the illegal immigrants? How many are there? Why do they come? Where do they come from? Where do they go and what do they do after entering the United States? Answering these questions is critical to understanding illegal immigration.

Illegal Immigrants in the United States

nexpectedly, the 1917 Immigration Act increased illegal Mexican immigration. Its tax and literacy requirements barred many Mexicans from immigrating legally, so they entered the United States illegally.

Many Mexicans left during World War I (1914–1918) to avoid being forced into the U.S. military, causing a worker shortage in agriculture and other industries in the American Southwest. The government responded with a guest worker program that allowed thousands of Mexican laborers to reenter. To ensure that they didn't stay permanently, the government retained part of their wages until they returned to Mexico. These events were repeated during World War II (1939–1945).

To fight illegal immigration, the Border Patrol was established in 1924 to secure U.S. borders. Efforts largely focused on the U.S.-Mexican border, although it's only about 1,900 miles (3,100 kilometers) long and the U.S.-Canadian border is about 5,500 miles (8,800 km) long. After World War II, fences and barriers were built

In this 1951 photograph, Border Patrol agents along the Mexican border watch and wait as a group of illegal immigrants approaches their vehicle.

along stretches of the U.S.-Mexican border in a failed attempt to halt illegal immigration. Some say the focus on the Mexican border makes sense because more people illegally cross that border than the Canadian one. Others claim the focus on the Mexican border reflects discrimination.

The Immigration Reform and Control Act of 1986 addressed illegal as well as legal immigration. Provided they had a basic knowledge of English and U.S. history and government, certain illegal immigrants received amnesty. Others received permanent status as part of a Special Agricultural Workers (SAW) program. In addition, the IRCA penalized employers who knowingly hired illegal immigrants.

The Illegal Immigration Reform and Immigrant Responsibility Act of 1996 (IIRIRA) provided for speedier deportation of illegal immigrants and prohibited them from applying for legal immigration for several years. It also allowed state and local law enforcement officials to help in the fight against illegal immigration.

Illegal Immigrants in the United States: Where They Come from and Where They Live

Because illegal immigrants try to conceal their status, it's difficult to know exactly how many there are. The DHS estimates that there were 11.6 million illegal immigrants in the United States as of January 2008.

Where did these illegal immigrants come from? According to the DHS, the overwhelming majority came from Mexico. The DHS estimates that more than seven million were Mexican. El Salvador and Guatemala contributed about five hundred thousand each. About three hundred thousand each came from the Philippines and Honduras. Korea and China each supplied more than two hundred thousand. Brazil, Ecuador, and India each sent more than 150,000. An estimated two million came from other countries.

Where in the United States do these illegal immigrants live? The DHS reports that California, Texas, and Florida had the greatest numbers. California's population of nearly three million was the largest by far. Texas had more than 1.6 million, while Florida had a little less than one million. Other states with sizeable populations included New York, Arizona, Illinois, Georgia, New

Jersey, North Carolina, and Nevada. Figures for these states ranged from more than six hundred thousand for New York to slightly under three hundred thousand for Nevada. An estimated three million lived in other states.

Why Do Illegal Immigrants Come to the United States?

The question posed by this heading really has two parts: what makes illegal immigrants leave their home country? And why do they come to the United States instead of another country? The second part is probably easier to answer.

The United States is considered a land of opportunity, where anyone willing to work hard can make a good life. People also believe the nation welcomes immigrants. The best-known expression of both ideas comes from Emma Lazarus's 1883 poem "The New Colossus," which describes the Statue of Liberty and appears on a plaque near the base of the statue. The last part of the poem is the most famous:

> . . . Give me your tired, your poor,
> Your huddled masses yearning to breathe free,
> The wretched refuse of your teeming shore.
> Send these, the homeless, tempest-tost to me.
> I lift my lamp beside the golden door!

Like these men, illegal immigrants often work as day laborers. They wait at selected locations for employers—like the men in the car—to approach them and offer work.

Now to answer the first part of the question: What makes people leave the only home that they've ever known, travel hundreds or thousands of miles to a country with a different language and culture, and start a new life, always fearing their illegal status will be discovered and they will be deported?

Most illegal immigrants flee war, starvation, persecution, poverty, and unemployment. Many leave their families behind and send a small portion of their wages back to them—about 10 percent on average, according to Aviva Chomsky, author of *"They Take Our Jobs!" and 20 Other Myths About Immigration.* Wages in the illegal immigrants' home countries are so low that these small remittances account for 50 to 80 percent of their families' incomes, says Chomsky.

Many illegal immigrants don't plan to stay permanently. They want to earn enough to improve their family's standard of living and then return home. However, the economic problems that began in the United States in 2007 caused many to abandon their dreams and go home. Others stayed because they can still earn more working here a couple of days per month in low-wage jobs than they could in their home countries.

Why Don't They Come Legally?

Why don't illegal immigrants apply for legal immigration? To answer that question, you first need to understand the system.

First, prospective immigrants must apply and qualify for a visa. That requires completing considerable paperwork and proving financial support, freedom from diseases, and a lack of a criminal record.

Second, U.S. immigration laws favor relatives of citizens and permanent residents, refugees, and people with skills needed in the United States. The Immigration Act of 1990 limited the total number of immigrants to

675,000 annually beginning in 1995. Of those, 480,000 spots were for relatives of citizens or permanent residents. Another 140,000 were for immigrants with job skills needed in the United States. The remaining fifty-five thousand spots were for diversity immigrants—that is, individuals from nations that had sent fewer than fifty thousand immigrants during the previous five years— with a cap of 3,850 per nation. (Based on the *2007 Yearbook of Immigration Statistics*, immigrants from Bangladesh, Brazil, China, Colombia, the Dominican Republic, Ecuador, El Salvador, Guatemala, Haiti, India, Jamaica, Korea, Mexico, Peru, the Philippines, Russia, and Vietnam were among those ineligible.)

These requirements disqualify a poor person with no relatives living legally in the United States and no special skills. Should a person be selected for a diversity spot, a prohibited disease or lack of financial support would be disqualifying. Even people who do qualify for immigrant visas may wait up to twenty years, according to Chomsky.

You might think that people fleeing war and persecution could enter legally as refugees. But the government decides who gets refugee status. Just like the people who qualify for immigrant visas, those qualifying for refugee status may have to wait years. In addition, the Refugee Act of 1980 limited the number of refugees that the United States would accept annually to fifty thousand (although the president can set aside this limit and often does).

Risks of Trying to Enter Illegally

Entering the United States illegally is risky business and quite costly. Usually, illegal immigrants pay a smuggler—called a snakehead by Asians and a coyote by Mexicans—to transport them. A coyote may charge up to $6,000, say Thelma Gutierrez and Wayne Drash, authors of the article "Bad Economy Forcing Immigrants to Reconsider U.S." Daniels reports that a snakehead may demand more than $30,000. To get the money, illegal immigrants might save for years, borrow from relatives, or work for the smuggler.

The journey is filled with danger. Kari Huus, who wrote the article "Illegal Chinese Immigrants Land in U.S. Limbo," reports that Chinese illegal immigrants might spend two weeks at sea locked in shipping containers aboard large cargo ships. Once a ship docks and the containers are unloaded, the illegal immigrants must pry their way out and try to escape without being captured. Illegal immigrants from Mexico and farther south may travel on foot or be packed into cars, trucks, vans, or buses. Sometimes, they're hidden in the backs of trucks between sheets of lumber or inside hollowed-out logs. Many can't swim and risk drowning when they cross the

Rio Grande into Texas. Gangs may attack them along the way. Coyotes may abandon illegal immigrants once they reach the United States, leaving them lost and helpless. Illegal immigrants crossing into the deserts of the Southwest often die of heat exhaustion and thirst.

Captured illegal immigrants are usually held in detention centers, sometimes for months. Dan Frosch of the *New York Times* reported on a study that revealed women in detention centers are often mistreated and denied medical care.

Federal agents arrest nearly 250 illegal Chinese immigrants. A cargo ship transported the men from China and then simply dumped them near San Francisco's Golden Gate Bridge.

Illegal immigrants who manage to arrive safely and find work often face poor pay and dangerous conditions. Their employers may hold them virtual prisoners. Illegal immigrants are often too fearful of being deported to complain or go to the police.

Do Illegal Immigrants Threaten U.S. Society?

As noted previously, the DHS estimates that 11.6 million illegal immigrants lived in the United States as of January 2008. Although the sheer number stuns many people, the debates about the effects of illegal immigration—and the open borders that help make it possible—are what keep the topic in the news. The principal debates center around the following issues:

- How do illegal immigrants affect the U.S. economy?
- Do illegal immigrants lead to an increase in crime, and does jailing those convicted of crimes burden the prison system?
- Does the added population resulting from illegal immigration harm the nation's environment?
- Do illegal immigrants bring cultural and language differences that threaten the unity of U.S. society?
- Does the fact that people can so easily slip across U.S. borders and enter the country illegally pose a terrorist threat?

On television and talk radio, you may hear heated, sometimes angry discussion about these issues. On the Internet, you can find forceful arguments about illegal immigration on the Web sites of individuals and organizations, including news organizations. People feel so strongly because they believe illegal immigration directly affects their lives. The terrorist attacks of September 11, 2001, and the economic problems that began in 2007 have heightened feelings on both sides of the issue and intensified the debates. This chapter will examine the issues one at a time.

Illegal Immigrants and the U.S. Economy

Many people complain that illegal immigrants harm the economy by using social services but not paying taxes. For example, the Colorado Alliance for Immigration Reform (CAIR) says the United States spends almost $7.5 billion annually educating the children of illegal immigrants and billions more paying for emergency room services used by illegal immigrants.

Others argue that illegal immigrants don't use many social services because they fear discovery and deportation. In addition, they're not eligible for most social services. If they have children who were born in the United States, those children are American citizens and entitled to the services.

Many also note that illegal immigrants do indeed pay taxes. Every time they buy gasoline or purchase goods, they pay taxes. Many illegal immigrants pay income taxes, too. In 2006, Mark Everson, head of the Internal Revenue Service (IRS), told Congress that illegal immigrants paid almost $55 billion in federal taxes from 1996 to 2004.

Numerous people maintain that illegal immigrants harm American workers in two ways. First, they take jobs from American workers because they're willing to work for less money. Second, they drive down wages. People who make this argument say illegal immigrants greatly increase the number of people looking for certain types of jobs (especially unskilled labor) and that drives down wages regardless of who fills the jobs.

Other people argue that these claims simply aren't true. They say illegal immigrants take jobs that Americans won't do. Americans refuse these jobs because they don't pay enough to live on, says Esther Cervantes, author of the article "Immigrants and the Labor Market: What Are 'the Jobs Americans Won't Do'?" Illegal immigrants who don't plan to stay, however, are often willing to live very simple lives while they're here in order to take more money back to their home countries, where it will go much further. In response to the argument that illegal immigrants drive down wages, many people say there is no research to support this claim.

Illegal Immigrants, Crime, and the Prison System

Some people contend that illegal immigration increases crime rates, especially in border communities along the corridors where illegal immigrants enter from Mexico. Sheri Metzger Karmiol's book *Illegal*

Here are illegal immigrants from Guatemala. The man at right works for a better life for family he left behind.

Immigration contains an essay by Stevan Pearce arguing that increases in crime near the border between New Mexico and Mexico are directly linked to increases in illegal immigration. Crimes include stolen vehicles, property damage, and drug smuggling. Violence related to drug smuggling has reached cities as far from the Mexican border as Chicago, Illinois, according to statements by Senator Dick Durbin that CNN.com reported. Some people believe that many illegal immigrants are involved in drug smuggling and that illegal immigrants commit more violent crimes than other groups do.

Others respond that there is no data or research to support claims that illegal immigrants commit more crimes. In fact, Jason L. Riley, author of *Let Them In: The*

Case for Open Borders, quotes studies showing that crime rates are actually lower for immigrants—legal and illegal—than for native-born citizens.

Those who claim that illegal immigrants commit more crimes also argue that keeping those convicted of crimes in jail costs federal, state, and local governments millions of dollars annually. Others reply that the percentage of illegal immigrants convicted of crimes and jailed is much lower than that of native-born citizens.

Illegal Immigrants and the Environment

One issue that comes up in debates about illegal immigration might surprise most people. It hasn't received as much attention in the news as some of the other issues, but it's an issue that greatly concerns some groups. It's the environment.

Some people argue that illegal immigrants cause environmental damage along the corridors where they enter. They leave behind a trail of trash that harms the environment, is unsightly, and places a burden on the communities that have to clean it up.

Others claim that illegal immigrants harm the environment by creating overpopulation in the areas where they settle. They further maintain that the increased population resulting from illegal immigration places ever-greater demands on limited natural resources in the United States, causing significant environmental damage.

People who oppose this argument maintain the evidence doesn't support it. Riley quotes researcher Steven Hayward, who says environmental quality in the United States has improved during the same period that illegal immigration has increased. Air pollution has decreased, the amount of forestland has increased, and farming practices that help preserve and protect soil are on the rise.

Illegal Immigration, Assimilation, and the Great Language Debate

Many people complain that illegal immigrants threaten America's cultural unity and, by extension, its health and prosperity. These people say illegal immigrants don't assimilate and often refuse to learn English. Some say this refusal to learn English is downright un-American—it rejects the language of the United States and represents a change from the attitudes of past immigrants.

Others argue there's no evidence to support these claims. Most immigrants, legal or illegal, who plan to stay in the United States do assimilate. As for immigrants rejecting the language of the United States, well, you should know that there isn't an official national language, although English is certainly the unofficial one. Besides,

These immigrants living in New York City show their desire to learn English. They are protesting budget cuts that threaten programs teaching English to immigrants.

there is considerable evidence that immigrants believe learning English is necessary and work to learn it quickly, even if they also want to retain their native language. Riley says the 2000 Census showed that 91 percent of Mexican immigrants' children spoke English well. Associated Press writer Deepti Hajela tells of immigrant fears that economic problems may lead to cuts in English classes. In an article in the University of Wisconsin-Madison newsletter, Brian Mattmiller describes a study that shows today's immigrants are much more eager to learn English than many past immigrants. Early immigrants often formed communities where only the native language was spoken for several generations.

Illegal Immigration and Terrorism

Particularly since the September 11, 2001, attacks on New York City and northern Virginia, some people have argued that the United States must do everything possible to prevent illegal immigration to protect itself from terrorists. Some say open borders threaten national security—terrorists may enter the country as illegal immigrants. Some claim that illegal immigration forces the government to spend resources addressing that problem instead of focusing on terrorism. Some maintain that illegal immigration feeds a flourishing trade in forged papers such as documents that can aid terrorists by making it easy for them to get forged passports, visas, and driver's licenses.

Others point out that illegal immigrants didn't commit the two largest terrorist attacks on American soil. The foreign terrorists responsible for the September 11, 2001, attacks entered the United States legally. Timothy McVeigh, a U.S. citizen who was born in the United States, served in the U.S. military, and considered himself a Christian, committed the worst terrorist attack on U.S. soil prior to the 9/11 attacks. In 1995, McVeigh bombed the Alfred P. Murrah Federal Building in Oklahoma City, Oklahoma, killing 168 people, including children. In fact, Riley says, not only did illegal immigrants not commit these terrorist attacks, illegal immigrants who entered by crossing the Mexican border—the focus of most efforts to close U.S. borders—have committed no terrorist attacks. Thus, even if illegal immigration across the Mexican border was stopped completely, there is no reason to believe it would protect the United States from future terrorist attacks.

Is Amnesty for Illegal Immigrants the Solution?

The idea of granting amnesty to illegal immigrants is one of the most controversial aspects of the entire illegal immigration debate, in large part because of the meaning and implications of the term itself. "Amnesty" comes from the same Greek word that "amnesia" does, and it means forgiving and "forgetting" past crimes—removing them from the legal record. For some people, the very idea of "forgetting" that millions of people have broken the nation's immigration laws is completely unacceptable. Even some supporters of illegal immigrants don't like the word because they don't believe a crime is involved, so there is no need to forgive or forget it. They prefer the term "legalization," which would change the immigrants' status from illegal to legal. So the debate over language continues along-side the debates over the issues surrounding illegal immigration. Because "amnesty" is the more commonly used term, it's the one used here. Although the debates sometimes make amnesty sound like a completely novel idea, it's not. Its history goes back much farther than one might think—to 1929.

The History of Amnesty for Illegal Immigrants

Before discussing particular amnesty laws, it might be good to remember that for centuries the whole idea of amnesty wasn't an issue. During colonial times, there were no immigration laws, so illegal immigration didn't exist. The Naturalization Act of 1790—passed only a few years after the colonies became the United States—was really about who was eligible for citizenship, not who was eligible to immigrate to the young nation. Restrictive immigration laws didn't actually begin until the late 1800s. Illegal immigration is possible only when such laws exist. And that's when issues arise about how to deal with it.

A 1929 law provided for a sort of amnesty. It allowed granting legal permanent resident status to any immigrant who was of "good moral character," was eligible, and had been in the United States since before a 1921 immigration law based on a national quota system.

As mentioned in chapter 3, the Immigration Reform and Control Act of 1986 granted amnesty for some illegal immigrants and created a Special Agricultural Workers program that granted permanent status to

The seated woman *(center)* waits anxiously as the man at left types her application for amnesty under the Immigration Reform and Control Act of 1986.

others, provided these immigrants had a basic knowledge of English and U.S. history and government. In 1994, Congress passed a bill that granted amnesty to 578,000 illegal immigrants. This provision was extended in 1997. That same year, Congress passed the Nicaraguan Adjustment and Central American Relief Act (NACARA) amnesty, which legalized nearly one million illegal immigrants from Central America. The Haitian Refugee Immigration Fairness Act amnesty (HRIFA) of 1998 granted amnesty to 125,000 illegal immigrants from Haiti. In 2000, Congress passed two amnesty bills. The Late

Amnesty legalized an estimated four hundred thousand illegal immigrants who claimed that they should have received amnesty under IRCA. The LIFE Act Amnesty granted legal status to nearly one million others.

As this list shows, Congress passed numerous bills legalizing selected groups of illegal immigrants through 2000. However, the terrorist attacks of September 11, 2001, dramatically altered attitudes toward immigrants among members of Congress and the public. Bills that included amnesty or guest worker programs failed to win congressional approval. President George W. Bush's Secure Border Initiative of 2005 contained a guest worker program that Congress quashed, although it passed other parts of the proposal. The Comprehensive Immigration Reform Act of 2006 (CIRA) would have created a guest worker program and provided a way for illegal immigrants to receive legal permanent resident status, but they would've had to pay $5,000 in fees and fines. Congress defeated it.

The heated debate over amnesty is far from resolved and will remain in the news for some time to come. So what are the points that people argue about?

Against Amnesty

People who oppose amnesty for illegal immigrants put forth numerous arguments to support their position. They contend that amnesty actually rewards breaking the law and is unfair to immigrants and prospective immigrants who follow the rules. Moreover, it will lead prospective immigrants to conclude there's no point in following the law, completing the long and difficult application process, and then waiting years for a visa to enter the United States legally. They might as well immigrate illegally. Amnesty will also encourage people who might not have considered immigrating to try illegal immigration. In the end, illegal immigrants would flood the United States. In addition, opponents point out, illegal immigrants who receive amnesty will then have one big benefit available to legal immigrants—they will immediately become eligible to bring their wives, husbands, and children to the United States, resulting in a significant population increase.

Opponents argue that amnesty presents serious, possibly dangerous consequences for the country. The financial cost could be enormous in terms of the benefits provided to the millions of illegal immigrants who receive amnesty and their families. The DHS already can't keep up with the work required to process applications for immigration. Granting amnesty would overwhelm the system and leave it unable to function properly, creating a national security risk. If the DHS can't sufficiently check the backgrounds of legal immigration applicants and the newly legalized illegal immigrants, who knows who might be among them? Terrorists and criminals might escape detection and be granted legal status.

Amnesty Is the Answer

People who favor granting amnesty to illegal immigrants have their own list of reasons in support of their position. The standard way to deal with captured illegal immigrants is deportation. People favoring amnesty argue that trying to deport all illegal immigrants simply isn't practical. It would require an enormous amount of time, effort, and labor to locate, detain, and deport them, and the DHS doesn't have a large enough workforce to do it. Some illegal immigrants would escape detection. Even if it were possible to locate and deport all illegal immigrants, it wouldn't be desirable. Whether people want to admit it or not, the truth is that the U.S. economy depends on the work done by these immigrants—particularly in agriculture, factories, and restaurants. Without them, the economy would suffer greatly, and everyone would feel the effects.

Amnesty supporters also argue that legalizing those who are in the country illegally would actually make the country more secure. Giving legal status to illegal immigrants would give the government records on and information about them, which would help it identify those who might be a national security threat.

These people are among about three hundred who gathered in Atlanta, Georgia, to protest granting amnesty to illegal immigrants. Their faces reveal their strong feelings about the issue.

In addition, making these immigrants legal would help protect them from being exploited by employers and would help protect their human rights—goals that are consistent with cherished American values. Amnesty supporters further note that illegal immigrants constitute a permanent underclass because they work in low-paying jobs and are sometimes mistreated, but they don't seek help because they fear deportation. Such a permanent underclass has negative effects on society as a whole. Amnesty supporters maintain that anyone who's been in the United States for five or six years, worked, paid taxes, and stayed out of trouble deserves the opportunity to become a legal resident.

Although amnesty is one of the most hotly debated solutions to illegal immigration, it's not the only one that has been proposed or the only one that has been featured in the news. The next chapter will examine some other proposed solutions.

Other Proposed Solutions to Illegal Immigration

While the heated debate over illegal immigration continues to capture attention, people on both sides of the argument agree on one point: Illegal immigration is a problem, and the United States needs to halt it. They may not agree on the steps to take, but they agree that something needs to be done. Possible solutions besides amnesty include the following:

- Stricter enforcement of existing laws, including deporting illegal immigrants
- Eliminating the open border between the United States and Mexico to stop illegal immigration from Mexico and Central America
- The creation of a national identification card
- The punishment of employers who knowingly hire illegal immigrants
- The creation of a guest worker program
- Change laws to allow more legal immigration

As with every issue surrounding illegal immigration, these proposals can provoke heated arguments that attract news reporting.

Stricter Law Enforcement

Some people argue that strictly enforcing existing immigration laws would largely solve the problem of illegal immigration. It would remove illegal immigrants already in the country and discourage others from trying to enter illegally.

Michael Chertoff, a former head of the DHS, believed strongly in aggressive law enforcement. One aspect of Chertoff's approach involved identifying illegal immigrants in workplaces. To accomplish this, the DHS created E-Verify, an online system that employers could use to quickly determine if an individual was authorized to work in the United States. (As noted in chapter 4, illegal immigrants can easily obtain forged documents, so employers can't assume an individual's documents are genuine.) The DHS aggressively promoted the use of E-Verify, and some states began requiring its use. The DHS also rounded up illegal immigrants in raids and targeted those who belonged to gangs. Those arrested went to detention centers.

Others have presented several arguments against this approach. Some have complained about the harsh treatment of those arrested in raids and noted that deaths have occurred in detention centers. Many maintain that the E-Verify system isn't reliable. Some argue that, no matter what the government does, there will always be illegal immigration, and trying to halt it completely would be excessively expensive. The government would need to hire lots more people and build more detention centers.

This businessman explains to Kansas legislators that the E-verify system is simple to use.

Various people favor training state and local law enforcement officials to identify and arrest illegal immigrants. However, others fear the training wouldn't be sufficient and could lead to racial profiling. Another controversial idea is that such people as teachers, doctors, and nurses should be required to report illegal immigrants.

The final part of strict enforcement of immigration laws involves deportation. Between October 1, 2006, and September 30, 2007, the U.S. Immigration and Customs Enforcement (ICE) deported nearly 277,000 illegal immigrants (including some who left willingly after their arrest). However, that is a very small portion of the estimated 11.6 million illegal immigrants in the United States.

In 2006, Tom Ridge, a former head of the DHS, estimated it would take nearly seventy years to deport all the illegal immigrants in the country, even if no more entered. He concluded that this approach wasn't practical or wise. The practice of deporting illegal immigrants also raises the question of what to do with those who have young children who are citizens because they were born in the United States. Is it right to tear apart families by deporting parents while their young children remain here?

Controlling the U.S.-Mexican Border

Because most illegal immigrants are Mexican and many from Central America enter the United States through Mexico, numerous people believe securing the U.S.-Mexican border can stop much illegal immigration. In fact, Alan Bersin, a former U.S. attorney, was appointed to the DHS in April 2009 to do just that. His responsibilities are to curb drug-related violence along the border and reduce the flow of illegal immigration. The problem, of course, is to find an effective way to do it. A favorite approach has been building fences and barriers. As chapter 3 noted, the United States first tried fences following World War II. However, their effect was limited. People simply found other places to cross, sometimes with deadly results. People entered (or were brought in by coyotes and abandoned in) remote desert areas. Many died from heat and thirst.

Even though fences and barriers haven't proven effective, many people believe they can be if longer fences are built and devices like motion sensors, infrared cameras, and unmanned airplanes are also used to watch the border. George W. Bush and Congress approved such a plan in 2006. However, the costs are very high. The year the plan was approved, Blas Nuñez-Neto and Stephen Viña prepared a report for Congress stating that 700 miles (1,127 km) of fencing could cost $9 million per mile, while the cost of maintenance over twenty-five years could reach $70 million per mile. These costs cover the fencing only, not the technological devices. In addition, people can still find ways around these systems. In fact, they already have. According to Senator Dianne Feinstein of California, forty tunnels

This tunnel under the U.S.-Mexico border fence demonstrates how ineffective such fences can be in controlling illegal immigration.

under the U.S.-Mexican border were discovered between September 11, 2001, and March 15, 2006.

Border security also requires people for surveillance and other tasks, raising the question of who should have these responsibilities. Some people favor using the U.S. military, such as the National Guard. Others oppose it, fearing increased violence in communities where soldiers are stationed. Some people prefer having civilian volunteer groups like the Minutemen patrol the border. Others strongly object, saying the group members are vigilantes, and they increase the likelihood of abuse and violence.

Other Options

A number of other options have been proposed to fight illegal immigration. Most of them have not received as much attention in the news as stricter law enforcement and border security have. Yet they're still topics that provoke discussion and debate.

National Identification Card

Some people have proposed a national identification card utilizing technologies like electronic fingerprints as a way to track illegal immigrants. They argue it's effective, uses technology that's readily available, and is affordable. Others say it's ridiculous to assume illegal immigrants who have already broken the law by their presence and who can or have acquired other forged documents are going to reveal their illegal status by obeying a law about a national identification card. They'll simply ignore the law or obtain a forged card. Some worry that a national identification card could lead to violations of the civil liberties guaranteed by the U.S. Constitution.

Whatever the merits of a national identification card, Congress and Bush approved the Real ID Act in 2005. Supporters of the act say it is simply a standardization of driver's licenses that requires all states to include certain information on licenses. Opponents say the law's real purpose is to create a national identification card.

Punish Employers

Some people have proposed punishing employers who hire illegal immigrants. The proposals range from fines to arresting the employers and charging them with a crime. The theory is that if employers pay a high price for hiring illegal immigrants, they won't do it. If there aren't jobs for illegal immigrants, they'll leave or won't come in the first place.

There are laws for punishing employers of illegal immigrants. However, they're not consistently enforced. When they are enforced, communities sometimes find that they suffer without the illegal immigrants and the jobs they were doing.

Guest Worker Programs

Guest worker programs are almost as hotly debated as amnesty. In fact, some people see them as amnesty under another name. Proposals for these programs vary. Some are directed toward seasonal workers, such as those in agriculture, and allow them to be in the United States for only a very limited time. All are based on two premises: guest workers perform jobs that Americans won't, and the U.S. economy suffers without them. Many government and business leaders strongly support such programs. As mentioned in chapter 5, Bush proposed a guest worker program in 2005, but Congress rejected it. Congress's reaction was in part a response to increasing complaints from certain groups of angry, fearful citizens who believe these foreigners threaten America's economic security as well as their own.

Relax Immigration Laws

Some people believe the best solution to illegal immigration is to greatly expand legal immigration. Jason Riley, author of *Let Them In: The Case for Open Borders*, contends that a more liberal immigration policy follows American traditions (remember, the United States didn't really begin to restrict immigration until the late 1800s) and maintains that all immigrants benefit the country. They keep the U.S. workforce younger and stronger than those of other nations. Because many open their own businesses, they create jobs. Since they buy goods and services, they contribute to economic growth. They make our economy more efficient and productive by taking jobs that Americans refuse.

These immigrant rights activists are taking part in a march in Seattle, Washington.

Riley further argues that allowing more legal immigration will reduce illegal immigration, which would let the DHS focus its attention on terrorists and drug dealers. This would make the country more secure than trying to locate and deport all illegal immigrants or block entry from Mexico with fences and technological devices.

The arguments over illegal immigration and solutions for it, including amnesty, aren't going away any time soon. They have been around a long time, and the country doesn't seem any nearer to agreement than it did a century ago. Yet illegal immigration is a challenge that the nation must face sooner or later. One can only hope that when the country finally agrees on how to deal with it, the voices of reason and understanding will overcome the voices of fear and anger.

Glossary

assimilate To become absorbed into a culture.

consulate The office of a government-appointed representative to a foreign country.

controversial Causing arguments and disputes.

detention The state of being held in custody temporarily by a government.

discrimination The act of treating a group of people badly because they are different.

diversity Variety.

documentation The act of providing official papers as proof of something.

eligible Qualified to be chosen.

finger scans Fingerprints that are recorded with an electronic device and used to identify an individual.

guest worker A foreign laborer granted official permission to work temporarily in a country.

literacy The state of being able to read and write.

naturalization The process of becoming a citizen of a new country.

natural resources Things in nature that people use, such as water, wood, and soil.

permanent resident A foreigner who has official permission to live in a country permanently, even though he or she is not a citizen.

persecuted Treated badly because of being different.

quotas Numbers or shares out of a total.

racial profiling The police practice of using skin color as a basis for stopping people.

refugee A person who has fled his or her country to escape war or persecution.

remittances Money sent back to family members in a foreign country.

social services Government-funded services meant to improve society's overall well-being. Examples include education, food stamps, welfare, and health care.

underclass The lowest level of society, composed of the poorest people.

vaccination A shot given to people to protect them from certain serious diseases.

vigilante A member of a group that enforces the law without official authorization.

For More Information

Americans for Immigration Control (AIC)

P.O. Box 738

Monterey, VA 24465

(540) 468-2023

Web site: http://www.immigrationcontrol.com
The AIC was founded in 1983 to stop the flow of illegal
immigrants from Mexico. It opposes amnesty and guest
worker programs.

Center for Immigration Studies (CIS)

1522 K Street NW, Suite 820

Washington, DC 20005-1202

(202) 466-8185

Web site: http://www.cis.org
The center is devoted to research and policy analysis of immigration's impact on the United States.

Citizenship and Immigration Canada (CIC)

CPC Vegreville

6212-55th Avenue

Vegreville, AB T9C 1W5

Canada

(888) 242-2100 (within Canada only)

Web site: http://www.cic.gc.ca

The CIC is Canada's official government agency that deals with applications for visas, immigration, and citizenship.

Federation for American Immigration Reform (FAIR)
25 Massachusetts Avenue NW, Suite 330
Washington, DC 20001
(202) 328-7004
Web site: http://www.fairus.org
FAIR believes that current levels of immigration are too high and advocates comprehensive immigration reform.

Immigration Watch Canada
P.O. Box 45075
Dunbar RPO
4326 Dunbar Street
Vancouver, BC V6S 2M8
Canada
Web site: http://www.immigrationwatchcanada.org
Immigration Watch Canada is a nonprofit organization that works to drastically reduce the number of immigrants allowed into Canada.

National Network for Immigrant and Refugee Rights (NNIRR)
310 Eighth Street, Suite 303
Oakland, CA 94607
(510) 465-1984

Web site: http://www.nnirr.org
NNIRR works to promote a just U.S. immigration and refugee policy and to defend the rights of all immigrants and refugees.

U.S. Citizenship and Immigration Services (CIS)

Washington, DC 20528

(800) 375-5283

Web site: http://www.uscis.gov/portal/site/uscis
The CIS deals with immigrant visa petitions, naturalization petitions, and asylum and refugee applications.

U.S. Department of Homeland Security (DHS)

Washington, DC 20528

Web site: http://www.dhs.gov/index.shtm
The DHS is an official government agency created in 2002 as a response to the terrorist attacks of September 11, 2001.

Web Sites

Due to the changing nature of Internet links, Rosen Publishing has developed an online list of Web sites related to the subject of this book. This site is updated regularly. Please use this link to access this list:

http://www.rosenlinks.com/itn/immi

For Further Reading

Becker, Cynthia S. *Immigration and Illegal Aliens: Burden or Blessing?* (Information Series on Current Topics). Farmington Hills, MI: Information Plus, 2007.

Guskin, Jane, and David L. Wilson. *The Politics of Immigration: Questions and Answers*. New York, NY: Monthly Review Press, 2007.

Kenney, Karen. *Illegal Immigration* (Essential Viewpoints). Edina, MN: Abdo Publishing Co., 2007.

Miller, Debra. *Illegal Immigration* (Current Controversies). Farmington Hills, MI: Greenhaven Press, 2007.

Newman, Lori M., ed. *What Rights Should Illegal Immigrants Have?* (At Issue). Farmington Hills, MI: Greenhaven Press, 2006.

Schulkin, Peter A. *Illegal Immigration: The Myths and the Reality*. Charleston, SC: BookSurge Publishing, 2008.

Stewart, Gail. *Illegal Immigration* (Ripped from the Headlines). Yankton, SD: Erickson Press, 2007.

Bibliography

Adams, Willi Paul. *The German-Americans: An Ethnic Experience.* Translated by LaVern J. Rippley and Eberhard Reichmann. Indianapolis, IN: Indiana University–Purdue University Indianapolis, 1993.

Cervantes, Esther. "Immigrants and the Labor Market: What Are 'the Jobs Americans Won't Do'?" *Dollars & Sense*, May/June, 2006, pp. 29, 30–31.

Chomsky, Aviva. *"They Take Our Jobs!" and 20 Other Myths About Immigration.* Boston, MA: Beacon Press, 2007.

Colorado Alliance for Immigration Reform. "Economic Costs of Legal and Illegal Immigration." Retrieved March 20, 2009 (http://www.cairco.org/econ/econ.html).

Daniels, Roger. *Guarding the Golden Door: American Immigration Policy and Immigrants Since 1882.* New York, NY: Hill and Wang, 2004.

Frosch, Dan. "Report Faults Treatment of Women Held at Immigration Centers." *New York Times*, January 20, 2009. Retrieved January 21, 2009 (http://www.nytimes.com/2009/01/21/us/21immig.html).

Gutierrez, Thelma, and Wayne Drash. "Bad Economy Forcing Immigrants to Reconsider U.S." CNN.com, February 10, 2009. Retrieved February 10, 2009 (http://

www.cnn.com/2009/US/02/10/immigrants.economy/
index.html?iref=topnews).

Hajela, Deepti. "Immigrants Fearful English Classes
Could Be Cut." *Buffalo News*, March 22, 2009.
Retrieved March 26, 2009 (http://www.buffalonews.
com/260/story/615754.html).

Huus, Kari. "Illegal Chinese Immigrants Land in U.S.
Limbo." MSNBC, April 18, 2006. Retrieved February 12,
2009 (http://www.msnbc.msn.com/id/12174500).

Karmiol, Sheri Metzger, ed. *Illegal Immigration*
(Introducing Issues with Opposing Viewpoints).
Farmington Hills, MI: Greenhaven Press, 2007.

Mattmiller, Brian. "Study Debunks Myth That Early
Immigrants Quickly Learned English." *University of
Wisconsin–Madison News*, October 16, 2008. Retrieved
March 22, 2009 (http://www.news.wisc.edu/15801).

Meserve, Jeanne, Mike M. Ahlers, and Carol Cratty.
"Senators Want to Fight Mexican Drug Cartels'
Expanding Influence." CNN.com, March 17, 2009.
Retrieved March 21, 2009 (http://www.cnn.com/2009/
POLITICS/03/17/mexican.drug.war/index.html).

Nuñez-Neto, Blas, and Stephen Viña. *Border Security:
Barriers Along the U.S. International Border*.
Washington, DC: Congressional Research Service,
Library of Congress, 2006.

Organisation for Economic Co-operation and
Development. "Glossary of Statistical Terms:

Immigrant Population." 2003. Retrieved March 4, 2009 (http://stats.oecd.org/glossary/detail.asp?ID=1284).

Ridge, Tom. "Immigration and Security." *Washington Times*, September 9, 2006. Retrieved March 25, 2009 (http://www.washingtontimes.com/news/2006/sep/09/20060909-101231-7134r).

Riley, Jason L. *Let Them In: The Case for Open Borders.* New York, NY: Gotham Books, 2008.

U.S. Congress House Committee on Ways and Means. "Statement of the Honorable Mark W. Everson, Commissioner, Internal Revenue Service." 109th Congress, 2nd session, July 26, 2006.

U.S. Department of Homeland Security. "Estimates of the Unauthorized Immigrant Population Residing in the United States: January 2008." Washington, DC: Office of Immigration Statistics, 2009.

U.S. Department of Homeland Security. *2007 Yearbook of Immigration Statistics.* Washington, DC: Policy Directorate, Office of Immigration Statistics, 2008.

U.S. Department of State. *Report of the Visa Office 2008.* Washington, DC: Bureau of Consular Affairs, 2009.

U.S. Immigration and Customs Enforcement. "FY07 Accomplishments." 2008. Retrieved March 25, 2009 (http://www.ice.gov).

Index

About the Author

Janey Levy, the author of more than one hundred books for young readers of all ages, is an editor and writer living in Colden, New York. She is a member of the American Civil Liberties Union, which works to protect the rights of all individuals in the United States, including both legal and illegal immigrants.

Photo Credits

Cover (top left) Joshua Lott/Getty Images; cover (top right), pp. 21, 29, 30, 36, 40, 47 © AP Images; cover (bottom), p. 25 David McNew/Getty Images; pp. 4, 6, 8, 33 Justin Sullivan/Getty Images; pp. 11, 13 FPG/Hulton Archive/ Getty Images; p. 16 A Description of the Immigrant Population, November 2004. Congressional Budget Office (http://www.cbo.gov); p. 19 Washington Times/ZUMA Press; p. 22 Loomis Dean/Time & Life Pictures/Getty Images; pp. 38, 44 Barry Williams/Getty Images; pp. 45, 49 Scott Olson/Getty Images; p. 53 Stephen Brashear/Getty Images.

Designer: Les Kanturek; Editor: Kathy Kuhtz Campbell;
Photo Researcher: Cindy Reiman